ONLINE
BATTLE ARENA
ESPORTS

THE COMPETITIVE GAMING WORLD OF LEAGUE OF LEGENDS, DOTA 2, AND MORE!

by Daniel Mauleón

CAPSTONE PRESS
a capstone imprint

Edge Books are published by Capstone Press,
1710 Roe Crest Drive, North Mankato, Minnesota 56003
www.capstonepub.com

Library of Congress Cataloging-in-Publication Data
Names: Mauleón, Daniel, 1991– author.
Title: Online battle arena esports : the competitive gaming world of
    League of legends, Dota 2, and more! / by Daniel Mauleón.
Description: North Mankato, Minnesota : Capstone Press, 2020. | Series: Edge
    books. Wide World of Esports | Includes bibliographical references and index. |
    Audience: Age 8–14. | Audience: Grade 4 to 6.
Identifiers: LCCN 2019005960 (print) | LCCN 2019006609 (ebook) |
    ISBN 9781543573664 (eBook PDF) | ISBN 9781543573541 (library binding) |
    ISBN 9781543574531 (paperback)
Subjects: LCSH: Video games—Competitions—Juvenile literature. |
    Video gamers—Juvenile literature.
Classification: LCC GV1469.3 (ebook) | LCC GV1469.3 .M3768 2020 (print) |
    DDC 794.8—dc23
LC record available at https://lccn.loc.gov/2019005960

Summary: Describes professional video gaming and game tournaments including
League of Legends, Dota 2, Smite, and more.

Editorial Credits
Aaron Sautter, editor; Kyle Grenz, designer; Tracy Cummins, media researcher;
    Laura Manthe, production specialist

Photo Credits
Alamy: CTK/David Tanecek, 4, 20; AP Photo: M. Spencer Green, 12; Getty Images:
AFP PHOTO/CHRISTOPHE SIMON, 6, AFP/ED JONES, 17, 27, Chung Sung-Jun,
22, Jeff Vinnick, 21, Josh Lefkowitz, 9, Mel Melcon/Los Angeles Times, 15, Suzi
Pratt/ FilmMagic, 18; iStockphoto: adamkaz, 26; Newscom: Daniel Reinhardt/
dpa, 29, REUTERS/Jason Redmond, 24; Shutterstock: EKKAPHAN CHIMPALEE,
Design Element, Eky Studio, Design Element, glazok90, Design Element,
Gorodenkoff, Cover Top Left, Cover Top Right, 5, Luca Lorenzelli, 11, Maryna
Kulchytska, Design Element, Phojai Phanpanya, Design Element, Rvector, Design
Element, selinofoto, 16

All internet sites listed in the back matter were accurate and available at the time
this book was published.

Printed in the United States of America.
PA70

Table of Contents

In *League of Legends* teams of players face off to destroy their opponents' characters and home base.

Welcome to the Battle Arena

The blue team brings another tower crashing down! They seem ready to make a push into the red team's base. The blue team's undead archer, furry sorcerer, alien knight, robotic doctor, and troll dancer gather together. As the players charge down the dusty middle lane, the sorcerer casts a spell, bringing fire down on a group of red **minions**. The archer draws his bow, finishing each minion with a single arrow. The knight, doctor, and dancer team up to defeat an opposing turtle warrior. Blades, teeth, and feet clash—and the turtle bites the dust.

minion—a servant or underling; usually with little strength or power

The blue team pushes forward. More trouble awaits as the players advance to the heart of the enemy's base. The sorcerer is taken out by a sneaky **assassin**. But the knight and troll get quick revenge for their fallen friend. The doctor casts a spell to heal his party. It has taken a lot of teamwork to get this far. To win the day they'll need to destroy the red team's base, which is heavily guarded. But if the blue team communicates clearly and times their attack just right, victory will be theirs!

assassin—a character who is skilled at killing others in secret or from a hidden location

In battle arena games, teams of pro gamers need to work well together to claim victory.

What Is a MOBA Anyway?

Multiplayer Online Battle Arenas (MOBAs) are a popular **genre** of video games. Each game drops two teams into a battle arena. The players select characters and work together to destroy their opponents' base. MOBAs test players' communication and strategy skills. These games have grown in popularity since the early 2000s.

> **genre**—a class or category; video game genres include role-playing, first-person shooter, adventure, sports, and others

In 2017 Misfits Gaming took on G2 Esports in a *League of Legends* finals match in Paris, France.

Hungry for competition, the best players participate in esports competitions. Esports events include tournaments large and small. Teams of professional players battle for real money and the pride of being the best players. MOBAs are incredibly popular. Millions of fans watch from around the world as pro gamers compete for millions of dollars. Get ready to enter the battle arena and learn all about the massive world of MOBA esports!

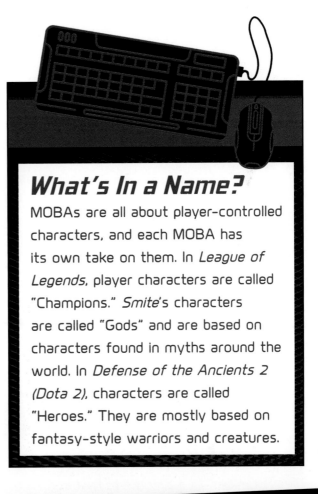

What's In a Name?

MOBAs are all about player-controlled characters, and each MOBA has its own take on them. In *League of Legends*, player characters are called "Champions." *Smite*'s characters are called "Gods" and are based on characters found in myths around the world. In *Defense of the Ancients 2 (Dota 2)*, characters are called "Heroes." They are mostly based on fantasy-style warriors and creatures.

CHAPTER 2

Tryouts and Tribulations

MOBAs are team games. MOBA players who want to become pro gamers need to join a team. There are a few ways players can find their place on a professional team.

Level-Up to the Pros

One game mode in MOBAs is called "**ranked** play." Players compete online against other players of the same rank, or skill level. The more games they win, the higher rank they can achieve. They might also watch videos of higher-level players to improve their own skills. One of the best ways for players to get noticed by a pro team is to keep winning and increasing their rank.

Fun Fact

Even before going pro, some players hire personal coaches to help them improve their game. Personal coaches may be former pro players or coaches, or even current gamers.

ranked—a game mode that keeps track of a player's skill level

Gamers at higher rankings may even compete against professional players. If someone gets to play against a pro, it's a great chance to show one's skills and teamwork. Beating a pro gamer is a good way to get noticed and to be remembered. When openings appear on a team, pro gamers could even suggest players they have battled against in ranked play. Today's opponents could be tomorrow's teammates!

Some of the best pro gamers started out by playing online to improve their rankings.

Smaller Tournaments

Players who want to join the pros often start small. They may play in small local or online tournaments to gain experience. These smaller tournaments can teach gamers how to play under pressure. Players often team up with friends they know or people they've met online. They might also create a blog or post their own gameplay videos. Hopeful gamers want to play really well, but they also want to get noticed as up-and-coming players.

Team Tryouts

Pro teams occasionally host open tryouts for hopeful gamers. Players can show off their skills online or by attending events in person. Tryouts are a great chance for players to show what they can do. Team coaches and managers judge players on individual skill and how they work with other players. Teams may also look at the players' rankings or watch recordings of games they've played in. If a player has an impressive performance, he or she may be invited to join a team.

Small competitions often host LAN (local area network) parties for gamers who hope to move on to larger tournaments.

Fun Fact

MOBA esports also has amateur leagues and tournaments. Newer gamers who want a taste of pro play can participate. Professional teams sometimes attend these events to scout for talented players.

scout—to look for players who might become professionals

Some universities offer students scholarships and equipment to practice their gaming skills for large tournaments.

MOBA Training

Pro players use a variety of training methods to prepare for games. They train alone to improve their own skills. They also spend time training with their team to learn each other's strengths and build winning strategies.

Grinding

Pro players can often be found playing ranked modes in their daily practice. Playing the game repeatedly to improve your skills is often called grinding. When new game **patches** come out, gamers can play in ranked games to practice any changes and learn new strategies.

Scrims

As part of their training, gamers participate in **scrimmages**, or scrims. In these games professional teams play against each other outside of official contests. Scrims are played with the full teams, which allow them to try new strategies for competitions.

patch—computer software that corrects or modifies a program or game

scrimmage—a practice game against another team or other players

Custom Game Modes

When practicing on their own, many players like to use custom modes. In custom games, players can change all kinds of settings. For example, they could start a match with all the best moves and items available to their character. Players can then try out new moves and strategies that may give them an advantage in competition.

Every MOBA game has unique features that are important to practice. Each team in *Dota 2* has small minions called creeps that march toward the enemy's base. By destroying an enemy creep, players gain both gold and experience. But one important strategy is knowing when to destroy your own creeps. Players want their creeps to do as much damage as possible. But by hitting their creeps at the last second, players can keep the opponent from gaining more experience and gold. *Dota 2* pros use custom matches to practice timing these last-second hits and gain a big advantage in competitions.

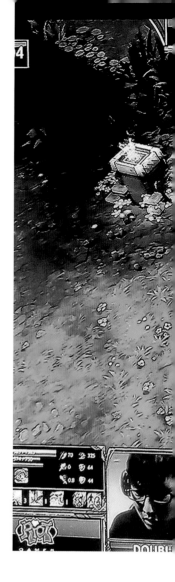

NA LCS SUMMER WEEK 7

	0/1/1	187		211	0/1/0	
	0/1/0	80		108	1/0/4	
	0/0/0	282		263	2/0/3	
	1/2/0	228		183	3/0/2	

COP

In *League of Legends* minions will attack any enemy unit they see. They also grow stronger the longer they survive in the game.

Fun Fact

Every MOBA game is different, but most feature some kind of computer-controlled soldiers. These soldiers fight alongside the characters and are usually called minions or creeps.

Replay-per-View

Pro players spend a lot of time watching game videos as part of their training. These videos on demand, or VODs, are usually recorded broadcasts of past games. VODs allow players to closely study the game. Players can play, pause, and rewind the videos as needed to track game statistics. This information gives players a better idea of their impact on the entire game.

Watching VODs helps players to study and improve their strengths and weaknesses. Maybe they did not time their attacks well. Or maybe they were at the wrong place on the map at a certain time. Team coaches review VODs to help teach the players and to prepare strategies for the team's upcoming opponents.

Fun Fact

Players often share their own VODs online. Gamers sometimes review others' gameplay videos and provide advice to improve their game.

Pro gaming teams spend a lot of time studying VODs to find weaknesses and create strategies for upcoming opponents.

CHAPTER 4

In 2014 LGD Gaming qualified for a playoff spot in The International Dota 2 Championships. The team finished in fifth place.

Winning It All

When a player finally goes pro and completes training, it's time to compete! MOBA competitions each have their own spin on esports, but they follow similar patterns. First, teams compete during a regular season to earn a spot in the playoffs. Once in the playoffs, teams battle it out to claim the championship.

Yao

Take Your Pick

Pro players can pick from tons of characters. There are more than 90 playable characters in *Smite*. *Dota 2* has more than 110 Heroes. *League of Legends* has the most with more than 140 Champions. Professional matches begin with each team banning certain characters. Teams often ban a few characters that the other team plays well, or characters that are considered too strong overall.

A Split Season

MOBA league seasons are usually split into two halves called splits. The first split is played early in the year, with a second split in the summer. The playoffs and championship games are then held in the fall.

During the regular season, teams earn points based on their wins and losses. Tournaments are held at the end of each split. Teams earn spots in the playoffs based on how they perform in the splits and tournaments. Sometimes teams might also compete in special events or last-minute tournaments for a chance at the playoffs.

Several pro teams competed in the playoffs at the 2018 Hitpoint Masters League of Legends tournament in the Czech Republic.

Global Championships

As with most sports, the playoffs are an exciting time for fans of MOBA esports. Each year millions of viewers tune in to watch the best teams from around the world compete for a championship.

Tournaments work in a variety of ways, but many take place over several rounds. In each round, teams face off in three- or five-game matches. Teams with the most wins move on to the next round and another tough match. Win enough matches, and a team can play for the championship prize!

High Stakes

The scale of a MOBA tournament prize changes depending on a game's popularity. In 2018 some championships were held as part of a larger gaming convention. Just eight teams competed for the title in *Heroes of the Storm*. The winning team, Gen.G, shared $500,000 in prize money. *Smite*'s World Championship series takes place in January in Atlanta, Georgia. In 2018 eUnited beat out nine other teams to claim the title and the $600,000 prize.

Thousands of fans packed Rogers Arena in Vancouver, Canada, to watch the grand final of The International Dota 2 Championships 2018.

Big Money

In the world of MOBA esports championships, *League of Legends* and *Dota 2* reign supreme.

The League of Legends World Championship has more viewers with more than 200 million fans watching worldwide. In 2018 the winners of the League of Legends World Championship won a prize worth more than $2.4 million!

China's team Invictus Gaming defeated the United Kingdom's team Fnatic to claim the 2018 League of Legends World Championship.

League of Legends is incredibly popular. But *Dota 2* is the king of huge prizes. In 2018 The International Dota 2 Championships were held in the Rogers Arena in Vancouver, Canada. The winning team received a grand prize worth more than $11 million! Even teams who fell short got a great payday. The team finishing in 6th place still won more than $1 million in prize money.

Growing the Prize

Dota 2 competitions can offer huge prize pools thanks to the players. Each year, millions of casual and professional gamers add to the pot when they buy battle passes. For just $10, a battle pass gives players special in-game items, different game modes, and other features to use throughout the year. For each battle pass sold, 25 percent of the money goes into the *Dota 2* prize pool.

CHAPTER 5

DOTA 2 CHAMPIONS

Commentators and game officials discuss game rules that players must follow at The International Dota 2 Championships.

Esport Controversies

Esports are great at bringing together players and fans from around the world. Unfortunately, there are times where players' attitudes and behavior can get out of control. Pro players follow rules set out by the game, the league, and their own teams. If they break the rules, they have to live with the consequences.

Reporting Rule Breakers

Riot Games often checks the game records of *League of Legends* players. The company enforces good behavior within their game. Being rude or verbally abusive to others is strongly discouraged. And purposely dying in the game or refusing to cooperate is also considered inappropriate. Players who break the rules can be fined for their behavior. In one month, a player's bad behavior was reported by others in 70 percent of his matches. He was fined $1,500.

Rules of the Game

Professional players need to follow certain rules of conduct. The rules cover many topics including rude language and behavior both in and out of games. Players who make offensive, racist, or sexist comments can face stiff **penalties**. Before a 2018 tournament in China, two *Dota 2* players made racist comments about Chinese people within the game. China's government banned the two players from the event, and both players had to pay a fine.

penalty—a punishment for breaking the rules

Inclusivity in Esports

During competitions, most pro gamers
are on their best behavior. They follow
the rules and treat others with respect.
But sometimes players let their emotions
get out of control. They may criticize their
teammates, use racist or sexist language,
or purposely insult others.

In the gaming world, the majority
of players tend to be young white men.
Unfortunately, a few of them have negative
attitudes toward women and people of
color. Their bad behavior makes the game
less enjoyable for both players and fans.

Team QWER is an all female team of gamers from South Korea. Just like male players, the women spend many hours intensely training for major tournaments.

Thankfully, fans want to see the best players compete, regardless of their sex or skin color. Esport leagues want fans to get the best competition possible. So they're working to stop bad gamer behavior. They can fine or ban gamers who **harass** others about their religion, skin color, gender, sexual orientation, and more. While this policy isn't perfect, it has been helping. In recent years more women and people of color are finding success within the pro gaming leagues.

harass—to purposely insult, bother, or annoy someone again and again

Until the Next Battle!

MOBAs are currently the most popular genre in esports. Each year more and more people play and watch MOBAs for the first time. It isn't quite a global pastime yet. But it's not hard to imagine a future where lots of people are buzzing about the latest big video game contest.

Players who want to go pro need to be dedicated to the game. After practicing online, they can attend smaller tournaments to show off their skills. If they are talented enough to join a pro team, the real challenge then begins. Pro players have busy schedules full of training and preparing for the next competition. But with a lot of hard work, gamers may get a shot at winning championship glory and huge cash prizes!

With tons of practice and teamwork, MOBA esport teams can reach the top and win a world championship title.

Fun Fact

Most MOBAs are played on personal computers. However, a few like *Smite* are available for game consoles like Xbox, Playstation, and Nintendo Switch. There are even a few mobile MOBAs!

Glossary

assassin (uh-SAS-uhn)—a character who is skilled at killing others in secret or from a hidden location

genre (ZHAHN-ruh)—a class or category; video game genres include role-playing, first-person shooter, adventure, sports, and others

harass (ha-RASS)—to purposely insult, bother, or annoy someone again and again

minion (MIN-yuhn)—a servant or underling; usually with little strength or power

patch (PACH)—computer software that corrects or modifies a program or game

penalty (PEN-uhl-tee)—a punishment for breaking the rules

ranked (RANKT)—a game mode that keeps track of a player's skill level

scout (SKOUT)—to look for players who might become professionals

scrimmage (SKRIM-ij)—a practice game against another team or other players

Read More

Jankowski, Matthew. *The Modern Nerd's Guide to eSports*. Geek Out! New York: Gareth Stevens Publishing, 2018.

Kaplan, Arie. *The Wild World of Gaming Culture*. Games and Gamers. Minneapolis: Lerner Publications Company, 2014.

Mauleón, Daniel. *Esports Revolution*. Video Game Revolution. North Mankato, MN: Capstone Press, 2019.

Internet Sites

ESPN: Esports
http://www.espn.com/esports/

Esports Earnings
https://www.esportsearnings.com/

Super League
https://www.superleague.com/

Index